1. Higgs

CILLA MCQUEEN

in association with the
ALEXANDER TURNBULL LIBRARY

OTAGO

Through waist-high grass cut through the empty section. Bend to retrieve the glossy supplement falling out of the newspaper. Slip ankle-deep in muddy water.

Jump the stream, land in tough bracken. A narrow track through lupins up the bank to the road, not a short cut.

ONE wet shoe, damp pages stick together, gold high heels dancing, a dress the colour of wild lupins, mascara, holidays, bin it.

Feel for keys, Braille-fingered
over pen, lipstick, purse, cards,
diary, paper-clip. Not a jingle.

Hurry back down the bank steeper from above, retrace the slippery track under the lupins, brush off lupin flowers in a clearing edged with serried russet stalks, no passage visible.

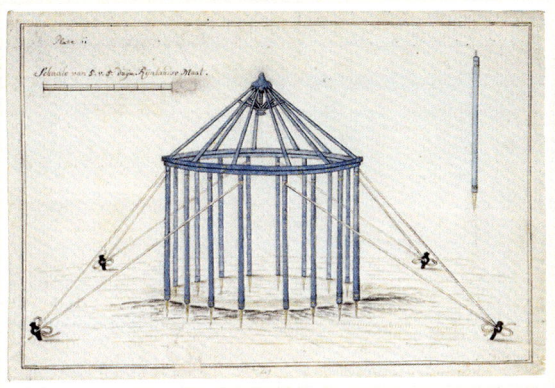

U̲ɴᴛɪʟ a tabby cat appears,
stares, disappears.

Find the opening, stride through tall resistance, arms covering the face; slide into the stream.

   The keys unseen. Nor palpable among the boggy roots.

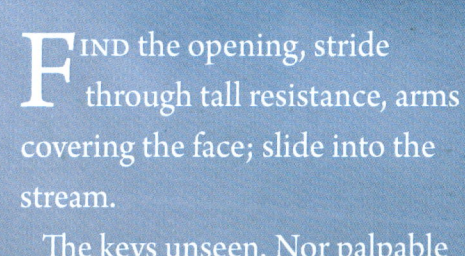

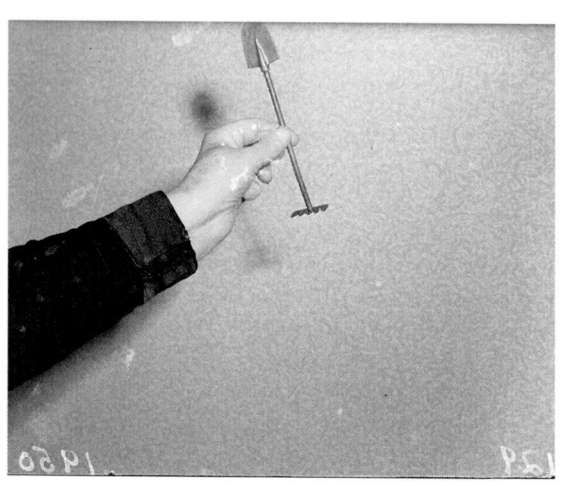

16

Go home. With a chisel ruin the frame, climb through the window.

A duplicate, a duplicate.

A cup of tea, make scones for Eric the Red who might turn up tonight with his telescope.

The almanac open at the page on Caelum, etched in the heavens between Columba and Eridanus.

Look up, affected by the gaze from the apple tree outside the window of the same tabby cat, or one similar.

N OUGHT but the grin etched in mind, the last miaow of Blossom who died bolt upright like a Queen.

Alpha Caeli, Eric states, has a diminutive M-class red dwarf companion in a very wide orbit.

Lacaille saw a pair of chisels tied with ribbon.

me-ow { Beneath the pale moonbeams misty light,
Just you and I dear.

W.G.B.

He cleans his glasses on his tie and puts them on again straight.

We might just be looking at NGC 1595 or NGC 1598!

THE scones are satisfying.

Murphy's particle, he repeats emphatically. You have to allow for the Higgs, sine qua non, absolutely nothing at all.

The more imagination grasps at the idea the greater the void created.

The arches of Eric's eyebrows uphold three horizontal lines across his freckled forehead. The wrinkles deepen as he glances up, keen-eyed.

Are you with me?

PICTURE CREDITS

Tussock grass plant *Aciphylla colensoi*. Pascoe, John Dobree, 1908–1972: Photographic albums, prints and negatives
Ref: 1/4-044636-F

Fox, William (Rt Hon Sir), 1812?–1893. [Fox, William] 1812–1893: Buller [1846?]
Ref: WC-325

Poul Gnatt and Julie Barker on sand dunes at Bethells Beach. Woods, Keith, 1928–1997: Photographs relating to dance in New Zealand
Ref: KW-0001-G

Paton, Harold Gear, 1919–2010. Flowers in fields near Sfax, Tunisia. Photograph taken by H. Paton, New Zealand, Department of Internal Affairs, War History Branch: Photographs relating to World War 1914–18, World War 1939–45, occupation of Japan, Korean War, and Malayan Emergency
Ref: DA-03012-F

Artist unknown: [Plan showing the structure of an observatory tent. 1769 or early 1770s?]
Ref: B-091-008

Ann Finnimore surrounded by vases of flowers
Ref: 1/2-147836-F

View of Mt Dumas, Campbell Island. Poppleton, Philip George: Photographs of Campbell Island
Ref: PA12-1423-012

Trowel for cultivating window boxes. Negatives of the Evening Post newspaper
Ref: 114/111/02-G

Study, Sir Frederic Truby King's house, Melrose, Wellington. Evening Post (newspaper. 1865–2002): Photographic negatives and prints of the Evening Post newspaper
Ref: PAColl-6301-87

View through a window, (Wellington?). Shotter, P.J.E: Negatives and albums (with index) of graves in the Bolton Street and Sydney Street cemeteries, Wellington
Ref: 35mm-25542-26-F

Old Man Rock or Queen Victoria, Puponga. Kent, Thelma Rene, 1899–1946: Prints and negatives of New Zealand wildlife and scenery
Ref: 1/2-009677-F

Maori needle, tatooing chisel and bird holding ring, alongside pieces of greenstone. Head, Samuel Heath, d 1948: Negatives
Ref: 1/1-007559-G

Baker, William George, 1864–1929: Me-ow. Beneath the pale moonbeam's

2. Hotdog

CILLA MCQUEEN
in association with the
ALEXANDER TURNBULL LIBRARY

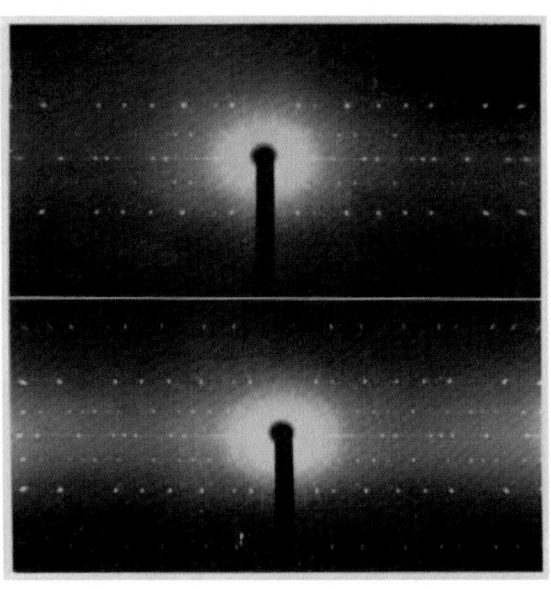

MARIE Curie stirred sludge in a cauldron with an iron bar as tall as herself, reducing pitchblende to a grain of light.

Pierre Curie's skull was eggshell on the cobblestones of Paris, thought Doris, flipping pikelets.

WATERBLASTER! shouted Roly. Three hundred, stainless steel tank, brand new. He put the box in the wash-house, pulled his hoodie up and ran.

It was too expensive. She didn't really need it.

At the dairy she was searching for eggs when Roly and his girlfriend came in and stood at the counter. The girl was laughing. Off the balcony!

I didn't undo the twists, Roly said.
Hotdog?

Green moss on the concrete, pine needles magnetised to the corners. Daisies. She put the radio on a stone and began gardening. It seemed the world was igniting in small puffs, bullet holes appearing in the Middle East.

A line of fire. She adjusted her glasses. Slowly tilting her head she gazed at the lobelia until at a certain angle through the lens the ultraviolet petals were thinly edged with red.

There was a spider dangling from her hat. She raised her hand to brush it off the brim but stopped, watching cross-eyed the minute creature climbing up. All elbows.

Waving the hat at the hydrangeas she went in to inspect the waterblaster.

It was only the size of a vacuum cleaner, smaller than the ones she had seen in Mitre 10. It had clean wheels but water dripped out of the hose. Looking for the guarantee she realised that there was no packaging and the box was battered.

T̲ʜᴇ serial number on the machine didn't match the number on the box.

No instructions, she thought, I don't know how to work it.

There was a deep scratch on the black plastic knob at the front. The power cord was tied with plastic twists.

Windmill. Oamaru. Built 1866. Pulled down. 1909. 68

Marie Curie remained radioactive long after her death, thought Doris, but she found the element she was looking for.

Trying to reduce the focus she scattered shells and stones from the

rockery. Something was stuck, the handle was leaking; one errant stream shot out of the side of the main jet.

The nozzle unleashed tremendous force in a gleaming nail of water that drilled into the Oamaru stone wall. Flowerpots skidded off a ledge and broke, scattering earth and polyanthus.

She slipped on the moss and the wildly swinging jet smashed the toilet window. She crawled to the outside tap and turned it.

Quiet. The wall drilled with holes as if machine-gunned. The drenched radio playing Tchaikovsky.

PICTURE CREDITS

c-axis rotation photographs of hyacinth from Snowy River. C. Osborne Hutton. Contributions to the Mineralogy of New Zealand—Part V, Volume 88, 1960–61, *Transactions and Proceedings of the Royal Society of New Zealand*.

Three people weighing and packing eggs. The Press (newspaper): Negatives
Ref: 1/1-008480-G

MacNab, Donald George, 1912–1996: [Painting for the cover of an unpublished book featuring paintings of the Napier earthquake. 1931]
Ref: B-155-023

Detail of a kitchen interior. Burt, Gordon Onslow Hilbury, 1893–1968: Negatives
Ref: 1/1-015728-F

The Petone Fire Station, with hoses hanging up to dry, after the fire at Bailey, Austin & Arcus timber yards, 1910. Godber, Albert Percy, 1875–1949: Collection of albums, prints and negatives
Ref: APG-0411-1/2-G

Couple with Frigidaire electric appliances in Wellington Botanic Garden. K.E. Niven and Co: Commercial negatives
Ref: PA12-3461-1

Unexploded Turkish shells at Gallipoli. Mackie album 1: From Egypt to Gallipoli
Ref: PA1-o-308-21-4

A village priest on his way to attend badly wounded civilians, France. Royal New Zealand Returned and Services' Association: New Zealand official negatives, World War 1914–18
Ref: 1/2-013148-G

Hodgkins, Frances Mary, 1869–1947: [Rear view of a man in doublet and hose, ca 1890]. Hodgkins family: [Album of sketches 1880s, 1890s]
Ref: E-312-q-091-4

Photograph of *Anisotome latifolia*, Campbell Island. Poppleton, Philip George: Photographs of Campbell Island
Ref: PA12-1425-060

Hutt Railway Workshops at Woburn. Interior view with new heating apparatus, 1929. Godber, Albert Percy, 1875–1949: Collection of albums, prints and negatives
Ref: APG-0891-1/2-G

Mayo, Eileen Rosemary (Dame), 1906–1994: Insect life [England, between 1926 and 1939?]: [Smaller works on paper. 1920s–1990s]
Ref: B-131-06-001

3. Birdie

CILLA MCQUEEN

in association with the
ALEXANDER TURNBULL LIBRARY

Doris looked up and cleared a swathe on the window. Mrs Good coming up in the rain, a baguette protruding from her bag.

No news but Olympics. Talking rubbish bins in Finland that speak with celebrity voices.

C ITY COUNCIL. The plot: from next year onwards those without reservations must go to town, not up the hill behind the pines. Gravestones on the sky.

A swooping plastic bag tangled in the fence, brushing off pink rose petals. If the wheelie-bin had a celebrity voice, in what language would it thank you?

Chicken soup on a day like this, nipping off a few dead buds.

A splendid concoction. Stressing the second syllable like Nigella Lawson.

Mrs Good at the gate, the baguette drooping. Hello sweetie, are you all right?

Fine thanks. You've got your bread wet.

Registered No. *Special*

Kimberley Supply Committee № 4044 B

PERMIT TO PURCHASE BREAD.

M *Hugh Ross*

of *Newywood Contgt*

is permitted to purchase *14* loaves of Bread for

Week ending _____ 1900.

John W. Dale

Issuer.

Did you know Digby who won Lotto and went out of control? They didn't find him for a week. Mrs Good straightened the bread. His daughter was out jogging.

N o chance with this hip, Doris thought. Two years jogging every Sunday with Roger until Edwin put his foot down.

O N TV a winner kissed his gold medal. An exhausted woman finishing the marathon wobbled and collapsed. She won't die wondering! shouted the presenter.

Dⁱᴇ wondering, repeated Doris,
leafing through the exotic birds.
Overdue. Her eyes stung. All gone,
feathers for hats, vanity, stoats, rats.

SHE turned to the smallest flightless bird in the world, seen only once and shortly afterwards dispatched by the lighthouse-keeper's cat.

An artist's impression showed the robust legs and soft loose plumage of the Lyall's wren glowing like a coin on a branch above a fairy prion on the forest floor. Two green geckoes and a lichen moth among the upper twigs.

The scientific world heard almost simultaneously of the wren's discovery and its disappearance. No sooner said than done. She blew her nose.

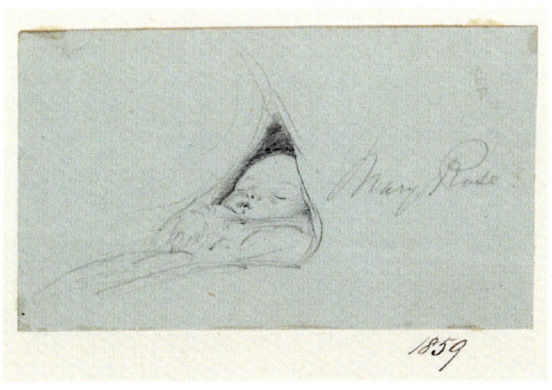

1859

Sky dark in the west. At the council office she filled out the form for a funeral plot. Ahead of her was the massive back of Mr Billing. He stepped backwards and crushed her toe, then nearly knocked her over.

She bought a cheese roll and sat on the seat by the rocks. Waves thumped against the sea wall. Sparrows and seagulls sought her crumbs. As she put the wrapping in the bin a seagull screeched and dropped a

white deposit on her arm. Thanks, she said.

It's lucky. A man was sitting on the seat, his parcels beside him. Lucky. Birdshit. Local? Shopping for one? None of your business, she thought, picking up her bag.

Sorry, he smiled. That was rude, nobody to talk to. I live up the street, said Doris. Nice to meet you. He was Digby's cousin, winding things up.

Drop in for a cup of tea any time, he invited her.

SHE remembered Digby with a glass in his hand on the porch of his weatherbeaten cottage. I don't think so. Is your bottle leaking? The brown paper was stained at the bottom.

S ound as a bell, he grinned, banging it down. There was dark liquid on the seat between them. Hell, soggy parcel, it's the chicken.

She took a tissue from her handbag and wiped a splash off her hand. Chicken juice, she said primly. Campylobacter.

Walking home past the native bush she peered under branches, listening to a bellbird's song. A sparrow hopped away through the leaves.

The Lyall's wren ran as fast as a mouse. Couldn't there be one pair left in the world, in some lonely place?

The letterbox coming off its hinges. I don't think so, she said in a loud, firm voice. Organised for survival, sound finances, even paid for the plot.

A man is so sudden, she thought.

I
N her quiet kitchen she remembered Roger's lavender bouquets and evening runs on the beach.

Edwin's blue eyes above his antiques book as she stood in the doorway ready to go out, toned and slim in her shorts, her brown hair soft and glowing like the plumage of the Lyall's wren.

PICTURE CREDITS

Women's Royal New Zealand Naval Service recruit learning semaphore on Somes Island. New Zealand Free Lance: Photographic prints and negatives
Ref: 1/4-000164-F

Modelling Jantzen bathing costumes. Burt, Gordon Onslow Hilbury, 1893–1968: Negatives
Reference Number: 1/2-036931-G

Mollymawk colony, Courrejolles Peninsula, Campbell Island. Judd, Norman: Photographs of Southern Islands; glass negs, photographs, postcards, all of Campbell Island; print of old hut, print of albatrosses
Reference Number: 1/2-100366-G

Miss Judy Young and Mrs W.M. Preston at Trentham race course, Upper Hutt. Negatives of the Evening Post newspaper
Ref: EP/1957/0298-F

Nelson Lighthouse, Boulder Bank, Nelson. Negatives of the Evening Post newspaper
Ref: 1/2-032647-F

Ross, William Burnett, 1908–1975. Kimberley Supply Committee: Permit to purchase bread. Mr [J?] Hugh Ross of New Zealand Cont[in]g[en]t, is permitted to purchase 14 loaves of bread for week ending ... 1900. G.A. Ettling, Printer, Kimberley. [Permits and tickets to purchase bread and soup during sieges of Kimberley and Beaconsfield (including Wesselton), 1900]
Ref: Eph-C-WAR-SA-1900-03-2

Creator unknown: Photograph of members of the Women's Royal New Zealand Naval Service, at signalling training, during World War II
Ref: PAColl-8844

Physical training at Sling Camp, Bulford. Royal New Zealand Returned and Services' Association: New Zealand official negatives, World War 1914–18
Ref: 1/2-014067-G

Running race for married ladies over 45, location unidentified
Ref: 1/2-C-016197-F

Hunting party, probably Christchurch district. Maclay, Adam Henry Pearson, 1873–1955: Negatives
Ref: 1/1-023909-G

Photograph of a city gate, Manila, Phillipines. Wells, Joan Mabel, fl 1986: Photograph album of Japan and photograph of Atiamuri
Ref: PA1-f-146-03-3

Rees, William Gilbert, 1827–1898: Mary Rose, 1859. Original sketches by W.G. Rees 1852–1884
Ref: E-199-q-041

Photograph of Richard Savage's watch. Savage, Michael Joseph, 1872–1940:

4. Inflation

CILLA MCQUEEN

in association with the
ALEXANDER TURNBULL LIBRARY

A CANTHUS leaves carved like lawnmower-tracks through the plush velvet of his armchair.

Most of his clothes were drying on the clothes-horse.

S TEAM rose from the socks.
Wavering upright in the draught, a white thread loose from a buttonhole caused Digby to imagine Jacques Montgolfier musing by the fireside at Annonay, smoking his pipe, tendrils of smoke drawn up the chimney.

LEANING forward, suddenly alert, to scrutinise a fine thread rising from the hand-made lace on Madame Montgolfier's lingerie.

Figs. V. and VI.—CHAIR AND DIVAN, exhibited at the Great International Exhibition of 1851.

S EIZED by the thrill of serendipity he tied the bloomers tightly at the knees and held them upside-down above the

heat. His thighs began to scorch. As the bloomers filled with hot air he appeared to be grasping by the waist a stout woman falling head-first down the chimney.

T̲HE early Montgolfière was made of silk and paper, Digby pleasantly recalled, and held together by one thousand eight hundred buttons.

Hot Air Egg. Blow the egg. Plug the hole at the little end with a dot of wax, enlarge the big end hole to admit a flame and voilà, up she rises, bobs against the ceiling.

He opened the fridge, shaking his head. Poor old Fossett. Bones, shoes, driving licence all over the Sierra Nevada.

P̲EARLED with dew, he thought, drawing on the cold glass with a fingertip.

The overgrown lawn glowed bright green. Spiro jumped up on his knee. Beyond the line of poplars to his right was the old water tower. See that? he asked Spiro. Just above that height Minnie Viola hit the cold air, poor girl, knocked the heat out of her.

A T LEAST she had her Moment d'Hilarité Universelle, he nodded, stroking the cat backwards. Good on her. Euphoria. Spiro jumped down and stalked away, stiff-tailed.

D^ORIS was passing the gate.

H<small>EY</small>, heard of Madame Blanchard? Digby shouted to her. Hey, how about setting off fireworks from a hydrogen balloon! Hubris! Doris shook her head and walked on.

Something fell from the branch above him. A small blue egg broke on the path. Reaching for it, Digby toppled into the hydrangeas.

WHEN he opened his eyes Doris was on the porch picking up broken glass. She looked annoyed. I left my keys on the kitchen table. I need to open a window.

Have a beer first. Just the one. She glared. Digby looked unkempt, for somebody who had won Lotto. You ought to be in the Bahamas.

Aftera few bottles he put the broken blue shell on his little finger and waggled it at her, grinning. Can't take it with you, babe.

The chisel made a mess of the frame. Crossly she thanked him and climbed in.

He tried to explain about the Montgolfière that carried a sheep, a rooster and a duck. How the sheep had pissed in the basket and was removed to Marie Antoinette's private zoo.

About inflation, but she clicked the window shut and drew the curtain.

PICTURE CREDITS

Drawing room, Government
House, Wellington. Ranfurly family:
Photographs
Ref: PA1-f-194-05

Beere, Daniel Manders, 1833–1909.
Steam crane, Gisborne, during work on
a breakwater
Ref: 1/2-096270-G

Chateau Tongariro, and Mount
Ruapehu erupting behind. Davis,
Bruce Valentine, 1913–2003:
Negatives of 1945 Ruapehu Eruption
Ref: 35mm-00702-a-F

Levien, Johann Martin, fl
1840s–1850s: Fig V and VI – Chair
and divan, exhibited at the Great
International Exhibition of 1851.
[1861]. The woods of New Zealand,
and their adaptability to art furniture.
London, James S. Virtue, printer, 1861
Ref: PUBL-0164-05/06

Stereoscopic photograph of a hot air
balloon over the Domain, Auckland.
Jeffares, Isaac Henry Bowen,
1868–1936: Photographs
Ref: 1/2-077688-G

Sewing kit designed to be presented
to every World War II soldier who
enlisted from the Wadestown district,
Wellington. Photographic negatives
and prints of the Evening Post
newspaper
Ref: PAColl-8557-71

Activities at Massey College. Negatives
of the Evening Post newspaper
Ref: 114/408/16-F

Buchanan, John, 1819–1898: Upper
Clutha Plains from a sketch by J.B. [ca
1860]. Scrapbook
Ref: E-208-q-008-1

Interior of a railway carriage, showing
several items of New Zealand Railways
picnic equipment. Godber, Albert
Percy, 1875–1949: Collection of
albums, prints and negatives
Ref: APG-2093-1/2-G

Mayo, Eileen Rosemary (Dame),
1906–1994: South of France [1947
or 1948]: Large works on paper,
1920s–1990s
Ref: C-127-001

Mansfield, Katherine 1888–1923
(Collector): Piece of K.M.'s yellow
silk dress
Ref: B-180-001

E-class steam locomotive Josephine, E
175, 0-4-4-0T. Godber, Albert Percy,
1875–1949: Collection of albums,
prints and negatives
Ref: APG-0234-1/2-G

Gondola-type ride at the New Zealand
International Exhibition, Christchurch.
Webb, Steffano, 1880?–1967:
Collection of negatives
Ref: 1/2-049706-G

5. Pleochroic

CILLA MCQUEEN

in association with the
ALEXANDER TURNBULL LIBRARY

The woman in the red coat walked away. Walter screwed up the paper bag and threw it in the bin. Waste of time.

Spray from behind the sea wall found the back of his neck and trickled between his shoulderblades.

A T DIGBY'S, sponging chicken juice off his jacket, he guessed at his bank balance. Three weeks at the most. The furniture had some value. The rest in the car.

T˙HE cottage had a numb feeling. The bedroom was clean, Digby's possessions in two suitcases beside the bed and on the dressing table. Jean had taken most of the books. All yours now, good luck.

Not much left of Digby, Walt thought, picking up a hairbrush. Only a bit of DNA. In every flake.

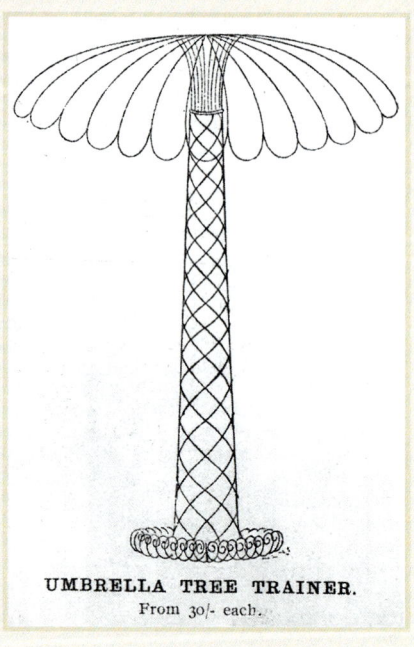

UMBRELLA TREE TRAINER.
From 30/- each.

H E put on Digby's glasses, frowned at the mirror and looked around the room, his sight enhanced.

F ROM the window he could read his numberplate. Plumes of spray sprang above the sea wall.

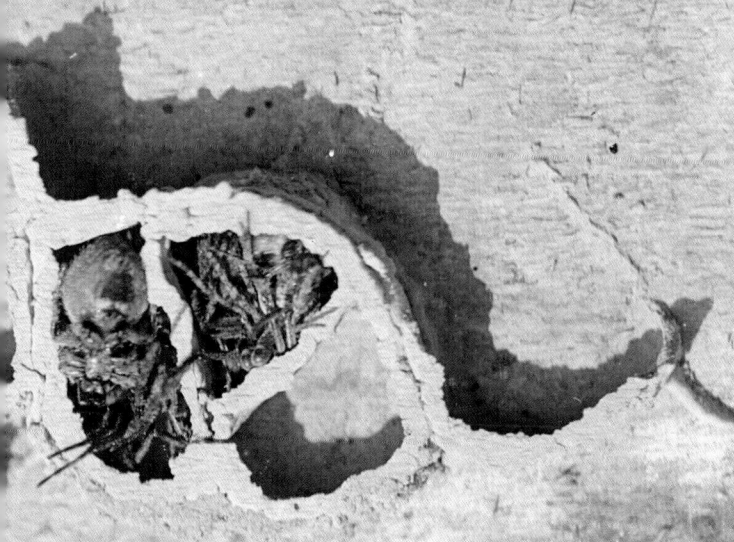

Hᴇ admired the markings of a moth on the window frame. Crepuscular.

Puffing dust from a book cover he recognised the fiery peacock colours of the Lightning Ridge Black Opal. The air spangled.

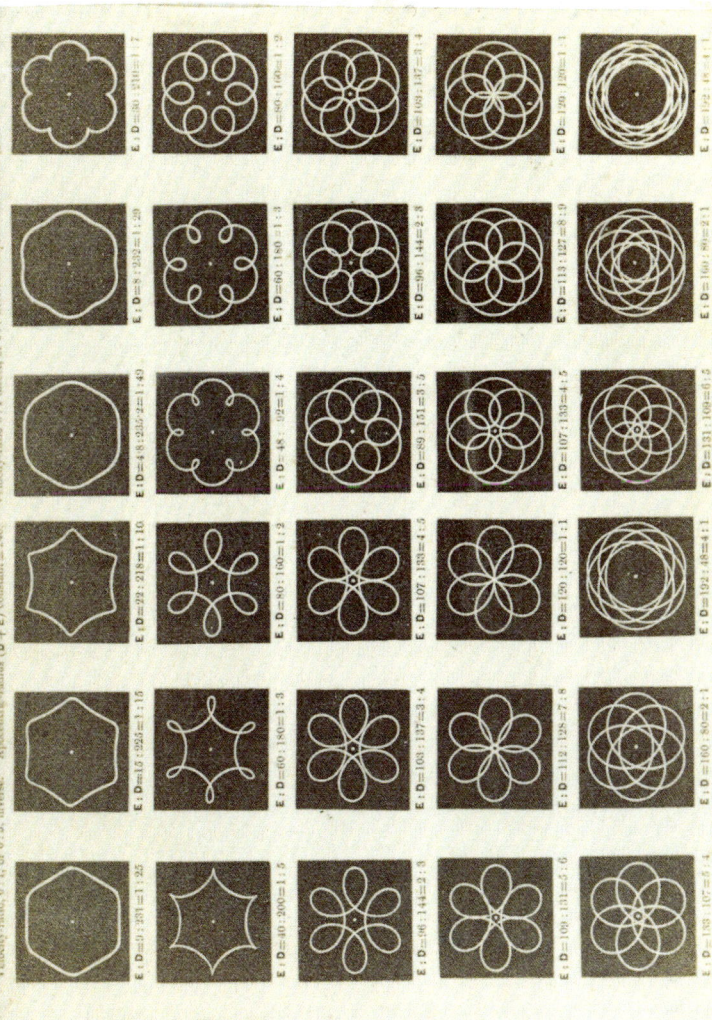

H E saw again the kindly, remote smile of his father studying rock samples with a magnifying glass.

Time out. He opened the wine and sat on the porch, leafing through pages. A feature of the chrysoberyl, he read, is the occurrence of twinned crystals in the shape of a heart, giving the mineral a pseudohexagonal appearance.

He grunted, recalling the last time he saw Beryl, asleep at her birthday table, her cheek resting on a pizza. He had closed the door gently and found somewhere else.

PLEOCHROIC Beryl, displaying different colours depending on the angle at which she is approached.

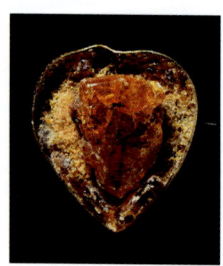

HIS voice startled a cat, poised half-way along the fence. It froze, its eyes amber crossed with gold; as it jumped down a blackbird fluttered away.

Alexandrite, he told the cat, was first discovered in the Urals on the day Alexander of Russia celebrated his

birthday. Alexandrite has the fascinating property of changing its colour from green to a raspberry red when viewed under artificial light.

H̲E took off Digby's glasses and the world softened.

Digby's bed had an electric blanket. Walt thought he should take the sheets off and use his own sleeping bag. As he removed the fitted sheet, a wad of money fell on the floor.

PERIODS		IMPORTANT PHYSICAL EVENTS	TIME IN MILLIONS OF YRS	IMPORTANT ORGANIC EVENTS
QUATERNARY	RECENT	YOUTHFUL LAND-FORMS RETREAT OF GLACIERS	2 M.Y. AGO	MAN ARRIVES IN NEW ZEALAND
	PLEISTOCENE	GLACIAL CLIMATE		GREAT ABUNDANCE OF MOAS
TERTIARY		KAIKOURA MOUNTAIN BUILDING	60 MILLION YEARS AGO	RICH SEA LIFE OF MODERN TYPE
		MARGINAL SEAS, CLIMATE MILD		FLOWERING PLANTS APPEAR
MESOZOIC	CRETACEOUS 70 M.Y.	FORMATION OF COAL	200 MILLION YEARS AGO	GIANT MARINE REPTILES ABUNDANT
		MOUNTAIN BUILDING		
	JURASSIC 38 M.Y.	NEW ZEALAND FORMS PART OF GREAT SOUTHERN CONTINENT		AGE OF AMMONITES
	TRIASSIC 32 M.Y.			FERN-LIKE & CONIFER FORESTS
PALAEOZOIC	PERMIAN 35 M.Y.	SUBMERGENCE	550 MILLION YEARS AGO	LAST APPEARANCE OF ANCIENT LIFE
	CARBONIFEROUS	NOT KNOWN IN N.Z.		NOT KNOWN IN N.Z.
	DEVONIAN 35 M.Y.	SUBMERGENCE		LAMP-SHELLS AND CORALS DOMINANT
	SILURIAN	NOT KNOWN IN N.Z.		NOT KNOWN IN N.Z.
	ORDOVICIAN 70 M.Y.	SUBMERGENCE		DOMINANCE OF GRAPTOLITES
	CAMBRIAN	NOT KNOWN IN N.Z.		NOT KNOWN IN N.Z.
PRE-CAMBRIAN		NO FOSSILS	3,000 MILLION YEARS AGO	NOT KNOWN IN N.Z.

L IFTING the mattress he noticed a slit in the bottom of the cover, closed with two safety pins. Inside among the complicated springs he felt a canvas bag.

A hundred thousand on the kitchen table and five hundred on his knee. The wine was nearly finished. From a standing start, he thought, the light has turned green. Out of it.

Red and Green Haiku
(by Walter, drinking wine)

"On a long drive alone, stasis.
A friendly wave from the Stop/Go man."

PICTURE CREDITS

Car number plate. Negatives of the
Evening Post newspaper
Ref: 114/274/09-G

Maker unknown: [Chinese textile
relating to Chee Kung Tong (Chinese
Masonic Society)]. Chinese Masonic.
[Masonic symbol with peacock
and flowers. Late 19th or early 20th
century]. Chung, Doris 1918– : [Eight
silk triangular Hung League–Chinese
Masonic Society regimental/ritual
flags with Chinese characters painted
on the front. 1925–1946]
Ref: F-089

Man and rocks. Negatives of the
Evening Post newspaper
Ref: 114/289/03-G

Kinsey, Joseph James (Sir),
1852–1936. Wilson, Edward Adrian
1872–1912: Sledge hauling on ski.
Mar[ch] 1911: [Reproductions of
Antarctic sketches]. 1911 [London?
1912?]
Ref: B-071-001

The Archibald Centre, Wellington
Zoo, New Zealand. Photographed by
Jon Hargest. Further negatives of the
Evening Post newspaper
Ref: EP/1990/3194/7-F

A.W. Buxton Ltd: Wire and iron
work; umbrella tree trainer [1905?].
[Ephemera and horticulture sales
catalogues issued by New Zealand
plant nurseries, 1900–09]
Ref: Eph-A-HORTICULTURE-
Buxton-1905-01-113

Albert Percy Godber's grandson
Norman Hartwig, on his 4th birthday.
Godber, Albert Percy, 1875–1949:
Collection of albums, prints and
negatives
Ref: APG-1464-1/4-G

Mason bees' nest. Price, William
Archer, 1866–1948: Collection of post
card negatives
Ref: 1/2-000628-G

Mathematical curves produced by
Henry Perigal. Craddock, Gerald
Rainsford, 1910–1990: Photographs
relating to the Glaisher family
Ref: PA1-o-190-10

James Hair's baby. Harding, William
James, 1826–1899: Negatives of
Wanganui district
Ref: 1/4-008218-G

Mansfield, Katherine, 1888–1923
(Collector): [Embroidered linen
bookcover, 1907–08]
Ref: B-180-003

McDuff, Laura, fl 2004. 1917 Souvenir
de France. [Embroidered postcard to
Olive McDuff from Lance/Sgt Walter
Henry Saunders]. [Ephemera relating
to World War I. 1917. Folder 1]
Ref: Eph-A-WAR-WI-1917-05

6. Tête à tête

CILLA MCQUEEN

in association with the
ALEXANDER TURNBULL LIBRARY

DORIS was transfixed by the bushfires.

When they were over she went into the kitchen to check the meat. It had shrunk. She hoped Walter was not a vegan.

Rinsing two glasses, she imagined herself incinerated by roaring flames as tall as a hillside.

As tall as a tidal wave. She would have to stock up against disaster. The tsunami pamphlet insisted on an escape route.

The quickest way up the hill would be through the gorse up the back. She should cut a track. Roly might be able to obtain an electric chainsaw.

SHE remembered Edwin on the day she found out about Roger, blossom flying everywhere. He wore on his head a handkerchief knotted at the corners and wielded the chainsaw with awkward violence.

MATCHSTICKS, said Edwin at last with satisfaction. No more apple pie.

He pulled off the handkerchief and wiped his face. Extinct.

S HE pressed one flower between two sheets of tissue paper and put it away in the dictionary. Nevermore, she whispered.

NEVER mind, here's Walter with his pinot, right on time.

When she opened the door he held out a bunch of pink hydrangeas. Voilà, Madame. Picked them myself. From Digby's? she asked doubtfully.

He followed her into the kitchen. There was smoke in the air. Are we having a barbecue?

J‍UST the roast, Doris apologised, turning the oven off. She could still see the victims. Negatives of a giant nuclear snapshot.

WALTER pulled two crystal glasses from his coat pocket and rummaged with the other hand. Gruyère in here somewhere. Corkscrew?

Humming off-key he leaned against the bench, watching her while she set the table. I am quite an aficionado of haute cuisine, he said, especially Nigella Lawson.

Doris was pleased she had bought a baguette. Nearly ready, she said. I want to make the îles flottantes.

A SPECIALTY of mine, he offered,
Allow me to show you how I break
the eggs.

One hand cracking, he poured the
yolk from shell to shell. Look, when I hit
the rim at this angle I achieve a perfect
equatorial division.

SNOWY peaks, pale gold sea, the islands like foam, dawn mist.

He poured another pinot. Ah, Dostoyevsky, he intoned, raising his glass. "We are like two abstract creatures in a balloon who have met to speak the truth."

PICTURE CREDITS

Firefighters at gorse fire, Silverstream. Dominion Post (newspaper): Photographic negatives and prints of the Evening Post and Dominion newspapers
Ref: Dom/1980/0902/01/08-F

Independent Order of Rechabites Friendly Society: No. 86 District. New Zealand Central. [Christ the Good Shepherd. Calendar]. 1908
Ref: Eph-D-ALCOHOL-Temperance-1908-01

Eagles Nest Geyser, Wairakei. Smith, Sydney Charles, 1888–1972: Photographs of New Zealand
Ref: 1/1-020257-G

Paul Cinquevalli. McAllister, James, 1869–1952: Negatives of Stratford and Taranaki district
Ref: 1/1-007889-G

Sawn logs, Northland. Northwood brothers: Photographs of Northland
Ref: 1/1-006269-G

Makara farmer Royce Brown spraying gorse. Photograph taken by John Nicholson. Further negatives of the Evening Post newspaper
Ref: EP/1980/0169/19-F

Men drinking a toast, and bicycle. Jones, Frederick Nelson, 1881–1962: Negatives of the Nelson district
Ref: 1/2-026145-G

Tempsky, Gustavus Ferdinand von, 1828–1868: The Queen Curasow. 1856: Attributed works: [Central American birds 1856?]
Ref: A-198-038

An older woman (possibly Laura Godber) partially obscured behind an apple tree. Godber, Albert Percy, 1875–1949: Collection of albums, prints and negatives
Ref: APG-1988-1/2-G

Dosimeter. Negatives of the Evening Post newspaper
Ref: 114/274/04-G

Display of decorative items. Burt, William Beverland, fl 1970s–1990s: Photographs of the Chatham Islands
Ref: PA1-q-041-frontispiece

Photograph of a Certificate in Anatomy, Physiology, Surgery and Dissection gained by surgeon John Dorset. Stout, Robert (Dr), 1882–1959: Photographs of papers and certificates relating to surgeon John Dorset
Ref: 1/2-012587-F

Match box showing size of meat ration. Negatives of the Evening Post newspaper
Ref: 114/261/13-G

Men competing in an egg and spoon race. Wall, John Reginald, fl 1890:

7. Nanoflowers

CILLA MCQUEEN

in association with the
ALEXANDER TURNBULL LIBRARY

Eric the Red scanned Births, Deaths and Marriages. So Beryl finally had her diamond ring. He closed the newspaper and folded it precisely.

Gather ye rosebuds, Beryl, not getting any younger. He remembered her waist that resisted his hands.

EGGTIMER. Preserve in waterglass. Seal the pores. He picked up a cracked shell.

Sands of time, Eric, Beryl murmured, painting egg-white on the petals of small flowers. Biological clock, you know? She sprinkled the flowers with icing sugar through a sieve.

Radiant nanoflowers, he said. Petrified violets.

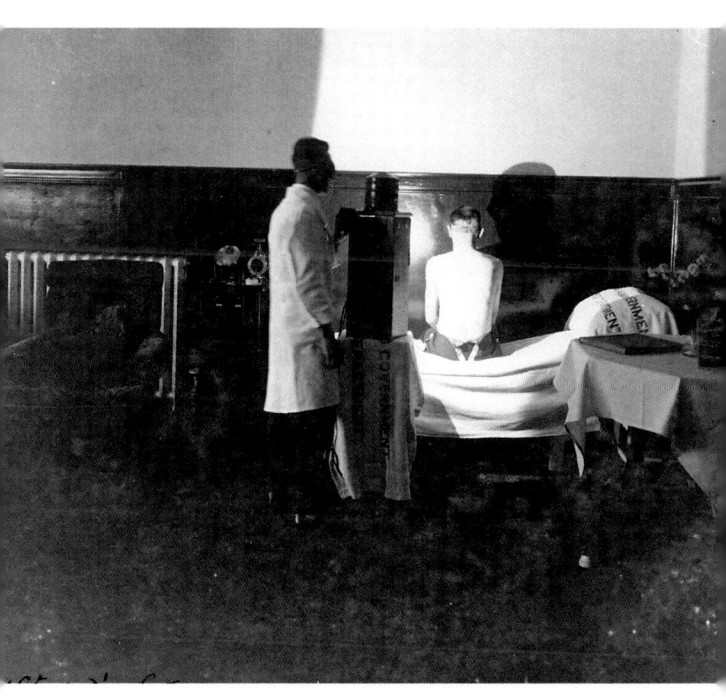

CRYSTALLISED. She crushed the eggshells in her hands and looked at him sideways. Don't let the witches go to sea.

THE vegetable garden demanded attention. Unthinned, his carrots grew twisted and shoulder to shoulder. Mandrake. He drew out one corkscrew-shaped, hairy, two-legged carrot, wiped off the earth and bit it. There was a tough yellow stalk inside. Too late.

Lately his thoughts had returned less to Beryl than to NGC2158. He wasn't sure he'd seen it. Whether what he had seen was NGC2158, because that was the night she had knocked the telescope askew. Since then he had searched in vain.

He looked up at the sky's blue eyelid, sealed by day and opening at night.

As usual on this date Eric remembered the Czar Alexander, with whom he shared a birthday. Who, he repeated, leaning on his fork, declared the miner's pick harder to wield than the sceptre.

H<small>E</small> winced. A pink potato impaled on the tine.

He stooped to examine a dead fledgeling among the onions. Its translucent eyelid was the bluish white of his mother's moonstone brooch from Peru.

Her voice was terrifyingly pure. Driving, his father threw back his head and accompanied her in a rich baritone that caused his eyes to water. Eric leaning forward in the back seat listened to their harmony in stereo.

He slipped the potato off.

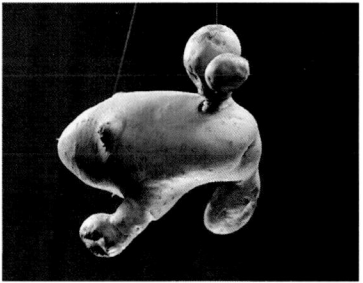

I<small>T</small> was soft-skinned, a black hole through it. Hole in the middle, he chuckled and sat down on the stump.

H E pulled the Tolstoy from his pocket and opened it at chapter 21. Smoothing out the corner of the page he read aloud, "'You must be a hole-worshipper. You pray to a hole,' retorted Nekhlúdov's driver, tucking his whip into his belt and adjusting the harness of one of the outside horses."

Pondering the probability of a torus-universe he continued digging. Emancipation of the serfs, the same birthday he met Beryl.

O BTUSE, he had thought. In the transition from observer to participant in her life, he had discovered her acute. Rings around him. Whether she had really gone to Siberia he didn't have a clue.

He viewed her distant profile, slightly tilted to show that she was listening, her eyes fixed on the road, hands on the wheel,

lightly as they picked lint from his lapel, brushed his shoulders, hovered over muffins depositing teaspoons of jam,

whipped egg-white into glistening peaks, made pastry for a bacon and egg pie, his favourite.

PICTURE CREDITS

Maker unknown: [Sumerian clay tablet with cuneiform inscription, ca 2250 BC]. Maker unknown: [Three Sumerian clay tablets with cuneiform inscriptions. Between 2250 and 2100 BC]
Ref: Curios-007-001-1

Stall at a trade fair showing the decoration on a cake that won first prize in the New Zealand Bakers' and Pastrycooks' exhibition. Price, William Archer, 1866–1948: Collection of post card negatives
Ref: 1/2-000269-G

Fragments of moa egg shell. Negatives of the Evening Post newspaper
Ref: 114/282/05-G

Ryan, Paddy: Dodge hearse owned by Boyd & Son, funeral directors, Martinborough
Ref: 1/2-181294-G

Ultra-violet ray, Sanatorium, Rotorua. Railways album 2
Ref: PA1-f-051-27-4

Prince of Wales' Feathers Geyser, Wairakei. Child, Edward George, 1860–1949: Photographs of the Ohingaiti district
Ref: 1/2-031979-G

Albert Percy Godber's grandsons, Colin and Norman Hartwig, with marrows and pumpkins, Silverstream. Godber, Albert Percy, 1875–1949: Collection of albums, prints and negatives
Ref: APG-1441-1/4-G

Three Russian refugees working at Griffins factory, Lower Hutt. Further negatives of the Evening Post newspaper
Ref: EP/1973/2603/23

Eclipse of the moon. Negatives of the Evening Post newspaper
Ref: 114/275/12-F

Hodgkins, William Mathew, 1833–1898: To further fields ... [ca 1890]. [Hodgkins, William Mathew] 1833–1898: [Sketchbook, one sketch dated 1864, one 1893]
Ref: E-014-q-1-024

Mounted deer's head, England. Royal New Zealand Returned and Services' Association: New Zealand official negatives, World War 1914–18
Ref: 1/2-014036-G

Marjory Smith with a large piece of kauri gum, Northland. Northwood brothers: Photographs of Northland
Ref: 1/1-006276-G

Electric Lamp House (Wellington): The Lamphouse Annual 1948–49. New Zealand's leading radio and electrical guide. [Cover]. 1948
Ref: Eph-B-RADIO-1948-01-cover

8. Edwin's Egg

CILLA MCQUEEN
in association with the
ALEXANDER TURNBULL LIBRARY

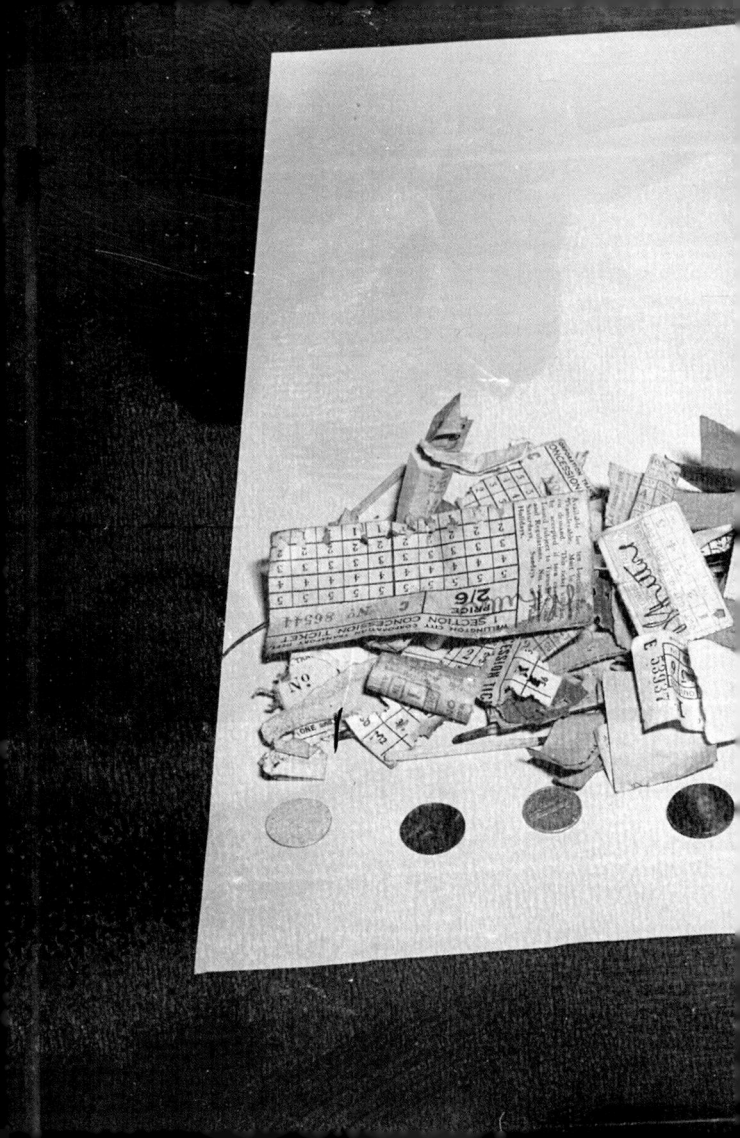

E<small>DWIN</small> gloomily sorted through the remains of his marriage.

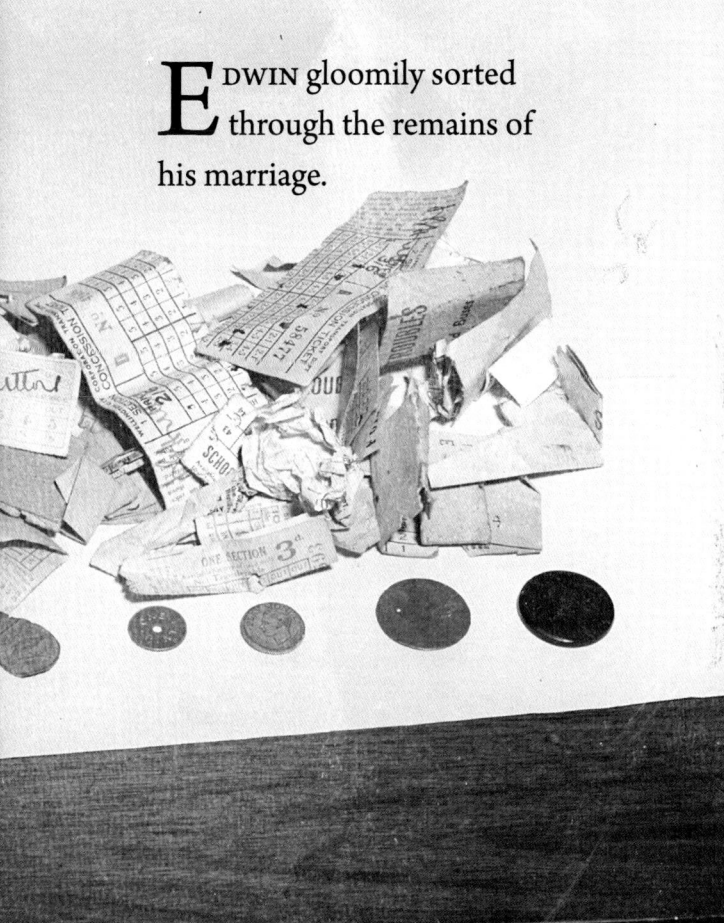

H E took a new cardboard box and wrote on the lid "Sporting Memorabilia". Then he turned to the shelves and took down one by one the tarnished trophies of his wife.

He wrapped them in newspaper and packed them in.

BOTANY.

Genera of Plants. N.º 4.

He paused when he came to the golden runner. She had not tarnished. Her limbs were as smooth as ever and as ever he bent his head and licked her little feet.

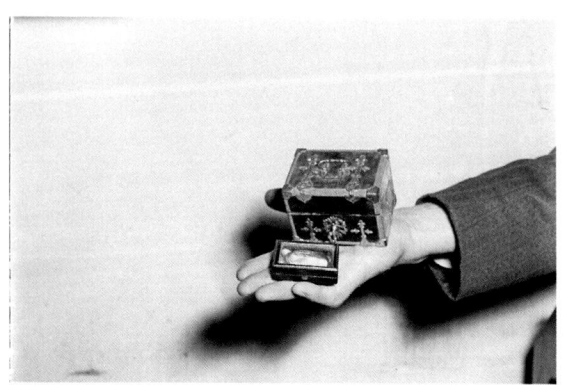

H<small>E</small> put her aside on the small table, beside the magnifying glass. After he had closed the box and stacked it with the others he picked up the magnifying glass and trained it on the green velvet chair.

WHEN he bent down to the chair with the glass to his eye he seemed to come into a green field. As he came closer he could see the stalks of freshly-mown grass. In places the grass was flattened and bent, flecked with wind-blown rubbish.

HE sat down. The bookcase was dusty enough to draw on. He drew a humpty-dumpty face looking over a wall, wide-eyed, knuckles on either side as if it had popped up out of the books. A single spiral of hair on the bald head.

H<small>E</small> blew dust off the carved lid of a lacquered box.

Inside was his wife's first artificial hip. The slim titanium spike gleamed. Ed pointed it at the window. It nosed aside the lace curtain and rapped on the pane.

R APPED again, harder. Two passing schoolgirls looked up, open-mouthed, turned and ran. One dropped her schoolbag, scattering things. Bent double she ran back, grabbing books, bag, pencil case, as if she were under fire.

On the radio in the kitchen Russia was invading Georgia.

He put an egg in boiling water, set the timer and made toast. By the time the egg was done there was a detail of soldiers on the plate, gleaming with butter.

Putting his tray on the small table he studied the bookcase.

THE larger books first. The Bible, for instance; the Wonders of the World, the Dictionaries, the Engines of War, the Nautical Knots, the Universe. Fabergé Eggs. He paused, opened it.

With the book propped against the golden runner he tapped his egg with the Apostle teaspoon then sliced off the top. The yolk, just hardened, remained a yellow dome. The white shone inside the top like the lining of a doffed hat.

THE Romanov Tercentenary Egg, he read aloud, chased with gold double-headed eagles and crowns framing eighteen miniature likenesses of Romanov rulers within rose diamond borders, rested on a pedestal in the form of the Imperial Eagle.

H is yolk was warm amber in a white crucible. He dipped a soldier in and sucked it.

Inside the Romanov Egg, a globe displaying historical maps of the Russian Empire, the landmasses described in gold on a blue sea.

H E smoothed the next page to examine his favourite. This was the last egg, the Steel Military Egg of 1916, surmounted by the Imperial crown in gold, executed in blackened steel and poised on the points of four miniature artillery shells.

B<small>ESIDE</small> the wartime egg a miniature easel, removed from within for the photograph, supported a painting the size of a postage stamp showing the Czar and his son in a grassy field under trees, conferring with the staff generals at the Front.

Edwin felt the menace of the egg.

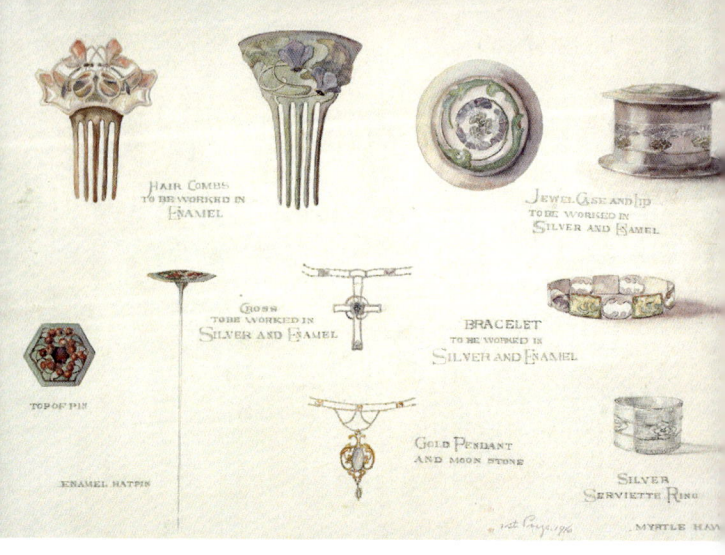

Not knowing it to be their last, the Czar, his son and staff, dressed in long coats and boots, discussed the battle. Meanwhile in St Petersburg the Czarina, as lovely as a quartzite lily, was conversing with Rasputin.

R<small>ED</small> and blue lights whirled outside the window. The silver Apostle flashed in the sun as it scooped the bottom of his egg, bringing out a curl of white. Lastly he ate the hat.

S OMEONE was making a noise down below. It appeared to be police.

The two schoolgirls stood at a distance, looking up. A policeman in the middle of the street raised a megaphone. Two others crouched behind a car. What next, thought Edwin. It must be the neighbours. The megaphone blared.

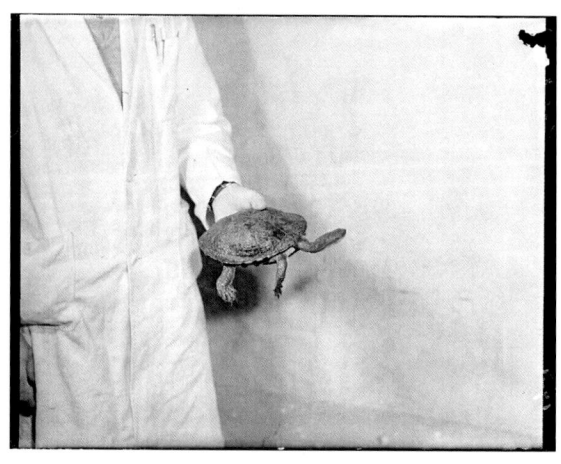

H<small>E</small> pulled the hip from his pocket and rapped on the window pane. He hadn't finished his lunch.

He turned the shell upside down, took out a black felt pen and began to draw the handlebar moustaches of the Czar.

PICTURE CREDITS

Contents of an honesty box on a tram. Negatives of the Evening Post newspaper
Ref: 114/356/07-G

Woman picking apples in the Nelson district. Pascoe, John Dobree, 1908–1972: Photographic albums, prints and negatives
Ref: 1/4-000984-F

Pass, J., fl 1790s–1820s [engraver]: Genera of plants. No. 4. Botany. Plate XIV. Pass sculp. London, J. Wilkes, August 4th 1799: [Botanical and zoological plates] London; J. Wilkes [1795–1800]
Ref: E-086-q-014

Field, Isabel Jane, 1867–1950. Hodgkins, Isabel Jane 1867–1950: [Study of a vase. 1880s?]
Ref: B-083-013

Exhibition at the Parliamentary Library. Negatives of the Evening Post newspaper
Ref: 114/258/03-G

Cigarette box presented to the captain of the English cricket team. Negatives of the Evening Post newspaper
Ref: 114/276/02-G

Egg standing party. Negatives of the Evening Post newspaper
Ref: 114/264/02-G

Living/dining room interior
Ref: 1/1-010493-G

Mary Elizabeth Dickie. Dickie, John, 1869–1942: Collection of postcards, prints and negatives
Ref: 1/2-034657-G

Allfree, Geoffrey Stephen, 1889–1918: [The evacuation of Suvla Bay. The burning of a million pounds worth of stores; last lighter coming away as dawn broke] 1915
Ref: A-176-003

Man with miniature radio. Negatives of the Evening Post newspaper
Ref: 114/227/03-G

Christensen, Edward Percival, 1907–1982. Christensen family breakfasting, Lower Hutt. Photograph taken by Edward Percival Christensen. Making New Zealand: Negatives and prints from the Making New Zealand Centennial collection
Ref: PAColl-3060-018

Youmans, Charlotte Beatrice, b 1869: Interior of St Pauls Cathedral, Wellington, 1896
Ref: C-119-001

Mason, Read Rex, 1904–1992. The Tell-U-Vision entertainer; the wrestling chart published to create a mind picture and increase your appreciation of the radio broadcasts / [illustrated by] F. Palmer. Printed at the Observer Printing Works, 12 Wyndham Street, Auckland. [1930s?]
Ref: Eph-D-WRESTLING-1930s-01.

Two eggs on a table. Negatives of the Evening Post newspaper
Ref: 114/257/13-G